anythink

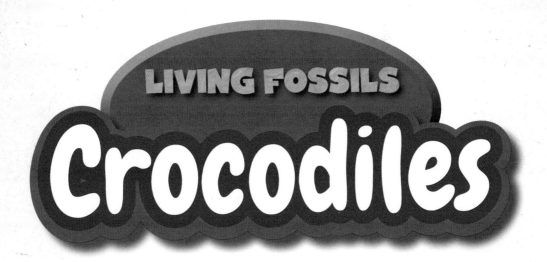

LIVING FOSSILS

Crocodiles

Therese Shea

PowerKiDS press.

New York

Published in 2015 by The Rosen Publishing Group, Inc.
29 East 21st Street, New York, NY 10010

First Edition

Editor: Sarah Machajewski
Book Design: Mickey Harmon

Photo Credits: Cover, pp. 1–24 (border texture) Markus Gann/Shutterstock.com; cover (logo texture), pp. 1–4, 6–8, 10, 12, 14, 16, 18, 20, 22–24 (background texture) Bplanet/Shutterstock.com; cover (crocodiles) Ronnarong Thanuthattaphong/Shutterstock.com; cover (forward-facing crocodile) nattanan726/Shutterstock.com; p. 5 Mark Hallett Paleoart/Photo Researchers/Getty Images; p. 6 (map) Kundra/Shutterstock.com; p. 7 (crocodile) Naypong/Shutterstock.com; p. 7 (alligator) Raffaella Calzoni/Shutterstock.com; pp. 7 (caiman), 21 defpicture/Shutterstock.com; p. 7 (gharial) Nazzu/Shutterstock.com; p. 8 worldswildlifewonders/Shutterstock.com; p. 9 Leonardo Gonzalez/Shutterstock.com; p. 11 Jonathan S. Blair / Contributor/ National Geographic/Getty Images; p. 12 Mark Deeble and Victoria Stone/Photodisc/Getty Images; p. 13 (top) Jeffrey W Lang/Photo Researchers/Getty Images; p. 13 (bottom) Trevor kelly/Shutterstock.com; p. 15 Myrna Watanabe/Photolibrary/Getty Images; p. 16 Daniel Rajsczak/Shutterstock.com; p. 17 MAHATHIR MOHD YASIN/Shutterstock.com; p. 19 Fotoluminate LLC/Shutterstock.com; p. 22 dioch/Shutterstock.com.

Library of Congress Cataloging-in-Publication Data

Shea, Therese, author.
  Crocodiles / Therese Shea.
      pages cm. — (Living fossils)
  Includes bibliographical references and index.
ISBN 978-1-4777-5816-8 (pbk.)
ISBN 978-1-4777-5815-1 (6 pack)
ISBN 978-1-4777-5820-5 (library binding)
1. Crocodiles—Juvenile literature. 2. Living fossils—Juvenile literature. I. Title.
  QL666.C925S539 2015
  597.98'2—dc23
                        2014029747

Manufactured in the United States of America

CPSIA Compliance Information: Batch #CW15PK: For Further Information contact Rosen Publishing, New York, New York at 1-800-237-9932

Contents

The Incredible Croc

How do you picture a crocodile? You probably think of its long **snout**, bumpy green skin, and thick tail. You probably don't want to think about its deadly bite! All these **adaptations** have helped crocodiles, a kind of **reptile**, live on Earth for a long, long time. Scientists have found crocodile fossils, or hardened remains, that are 200 million years old!

The crocodiles we see today are much like those that lived 80 million years ago. That's why crocodiles are said to be living fossils. In this book, we'll find out why crocodiles are supersurvivors.

The crocodiles (or "crocs" for short) of today are much like the crocs that lived alongside dinosaurs!

4

True Crocodiles

Crocodiles belong to an animal group called Crocodylia (krah-kuh-DIHL-ee-yuh). There are 23 species, or kinds, of "crocodilians" in this group, including alligators, caimans, gharials, and "true crocodiles." There are 14 species of true crocodiles.

All true crocodiles live in warm, wet **habitats**. They can walk on land, but they spend most of their time in water. Some crocodiles live in salt water, while others live in **brackish** water or freshwater.

North America

Europe   Asia

Africa

South America

Australia

crocodile zones

FOSSIL FACTS

South Florida is the only place where both alligators and crocodiles live.

Crocodile species can look and act differently. For example, the saltwater crocodile is the largest reptile on Earth. Many think it's the croc most likely to attack people. However, the American crocodile is smaller and shy.

crocodile

alligator

These creatures belong to the same animal group, but they're different species of crocodilians.

caiman

gharial

Spot the Croc

All true crocodiles have a long body, short legs, and a tail that makes them powerful swimmers. Their thick, tough skin is covered with scales. A croc's nose, eyes, and ears are high on its head. This allows a crocodile to smell, see, and hear when the rest of its body is hidden underwater.

How can you tell a true crocodile from another crocodilian? Crocodiles often have a longer snout that's shaped like the letter V. Also, the fourth tooth in a crocodile's lower jaw is usually showing when the croc's mouth is closed.

FOSSIL FACTS

Some species of crocodiles have more than 100 teeth! Crocodiles grow new teeth that force the older ones out.

Most of this croc's body is hidden underwater. Hiding is one thing that makes crocodiles great hunters.

The Crocodile Life Cycle

All animals go through a life cycle. The cycle is a number of events that happen between birth and death, including **mating** and making new life.

A baby croc's life begins as an egg. A mother croc lays up to 50 hard-shelled eggs in a nest near water. Croc nests can be different. Nile crocodiles dig holes in the ground to make nests. They cover their eggs with dirt. Saltwater crocodiles build nests of dirt and plants. Heat from the sun and rotting plants keeps the eggs warm.

FOSSIL FACTS

The **temperature** in a croc nest can affect whether babies are male or female.

In this photograph, a mother crocodile tends to her eggs while the father crocodile stands guard.

Aw! Baby Crocs

After 2 or 3 months, the baby crocs are ready to hatch, or break out of their eggs. They make noises that their mother can hear. She helps the baby crocodiles, or hatchlings, into the water. Then the mother crocodile may look after the hatchlings for a time, depending on the species.

Once grown, crocodiles spend most of their time alone. Males and females come together once a year to mate, though. This starts the croc life cycle again. Most crocodiles live 50 to 75 years. However, Nile crocodiles may live as long as 80 years.

A mother crocodile may help break open her eggs with her tongue. She may carry her hatchlings to the water in her mouth, too!

Cold-Blooded Sunbathers

Crocodiles are cold-blooded. That means their inner body temperature changes with their surroundings. On warm days, crocodiles may lay in the sun to take in heat. When they get too warm, they move to shade or enter the water. Crocs can be spotted with their mouth open. This is another way of cooling off.

Being cold-blooded is another reason why crocs have survived for so long. Cold-blooded animals don't need to eat to keep up their body temperature. Their bodies store food and use it later. Warm-blooded animals, such as people, can't survive like this.

FOSSIL FACTS

Crocs can go for a year without eating! However, most eat about 50 times a year.

Some crocodiles dig dens, or burrows, near lakes and rivers that fill with water. Burrows help crocs hide and guard themselves from heat, cold, and dry weather.

Croc Attack!

Crocodiles are mostly active at night. They have a special kind of sight that helps them see well in darkness. They also have tiny pits in the skin around their mouth that sense movements in the water. This helps them find **prey**, even when it's dark.

To catch animals on land, a crocodile floats at the water's edge. When prey comes to drink, the croc dives forward and bites it. If a crocodile's prey is large, the croc may grab part of its body and spin around and around in the water to tear the prey apart!

FOSSIL FACTS

Crocs aren't picky eaters! Their tough stomach can break down bones, horns, hoofs, and shells. This is one thing that has helped them survive.

Crocodiles eat mostly fish, waterbirds, and mammals. However, they'll eat just about anything they find.

Crocs on Top

Crocodiles are scary predators, but does anything eat them? Crocodile hatchlings are eaten by fish, birds, lizards, and other crocodiles. In fact, most hatchlings are eaten before they turn 1! However, adult crocodiles are at the top of their food chain. No other wild animals eat them. That's another reason they've survived for so long.

However, crocs have much to fear from people. That's because people have hunted crocodiles for many years. Croc skin is used to make leather for bags, shoes, and belts. Some people even eat crocodile meat.

FOSSIL FACTS

Not much harms crocodiles—they can survive even if they lose a limb or their tail.

Crocodiles' biggest **threat** may be people who build on or near their natural habitats, giving them fewer places to live.

Save the Crocodile!

Although crocodiles have small brains, scientists think they're the smartest reptiles. They seem to be able to learn. Sadly, some species of crocodiles are in danger of becoming **extinct**, even after millions of years of survival. It's not because of anything in nature, but because of people's actions.

Though there are now laws to keep crocodiles safe from people, illegal hunting and trading still take place. Building and **pollution** still affect habitats. Species in danger of extinction include the Orinoco crocodile, the Philippines crocodile, and the Siamese crocodile.

FOSSIL FACTS

Crocs don't often attack people, but it's a good idea to stay away from where they're found.

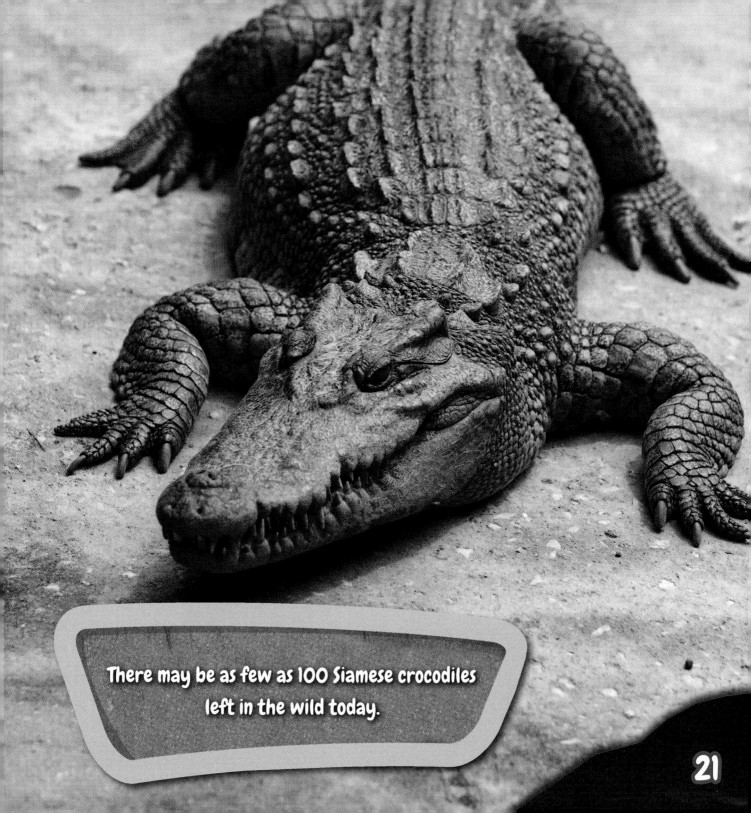

There may be as few as 100 Siamese crocodiles
left in the wild today.

Supersurvivors

Why didn't crocodiles die out like their fellow reptiles, the dinosaurs? Scientists have a few guesses. They think crocodiles can shut down their body systems when they need to. This helps them stay alive when it's too cold or there's little to eat. Also, crocs will eat just about anything. If something they ate died out, they'd just eat something else.

If there's any animal that will live millions of years more, it's the crocodile—a very cool living fossil!

Glossary

adaptation: A change in a living thing that helps it live better in its habitat.

brackish: Slightly salty.

extinct: No longer existing.

habitat: The natural place where a plant or animal lives.

mammal: A warm-blooded animal that has a backbone and hair, breathes air, and feeds milk to its young.

mate: To come together to make babies.

pollution: Harmful matter or chemicals that are put into air and water.

prey: An animal that is hunted by other animals for food.

reptile: An animal covered with scales or plates that breathes air, has a backbone, and lays eggs, such as a turtle, snake, lizard, or crocodile.

snout: The nose and mouth of an animal that sticks out in front of its face.

temperature: How hot or cold something is.

threat: Something likely to cause harm.

Index

B

babies, 10, 12
bite, 4, 16
burrows, 15

C

cold-blooded, 14
Crocodylia, 6

E

eggs, 10, 11, 12, 13

H

habitats, 6, 19, 20
hatchlings, 12, 13, 18

M

mating, 10, 12
mother, 10, 11, 12, 13

N

nests, 10, 11

P

people, 7, 14, 18,
    19, 20
predators, 11, 18
prey, 16

R

reptile, 4, 7, 20, 22

S

skin, 4, 8, 16, 18
snout, 4, 8
species, 6, 7, 8, 12, 20

T

tail, 4, 8, 18
teeth, 8
temperature, 10, 14

Websites

Due to the changing nature of Internet links, PowerKids Press has developed an online list of websites related to the subject of this book. This site is updated regularly. Please use this link to access the list: www.powerkidslinks.com/fos/croc